Entrepreneur Perspective on Product Management for AI & Data Science

By Sajid Inayat

1

TABLE OF CONTENT

Introduction/Overview

Is there a way start-ups and entrepreneurial will flourish in a future driven by machine learning and intense use of artificial intelligence? From SIRI to driving self-driving cars, artificial intelligence is gradually becoming the norm. There has been a whole new conversation on how artificial intelligence will disrupt a lot of occupations, for example, medicine, finance, taxi driver, etc. However, with such prediction, little attention is being given to entrepreneurship opportunities. A lot of people today see these technologies as a strange mystical magic box.

A lot of leading companies all over the world (Facebook, Google, Amazon) are really investing in artificial intelligence circle. A considerable number of these companies started in a small garage with ideas and passion, with a lot motivated by the thrill of doing something that has never been done before. The competitive advantage has long been linked to the capacity of America to innovate. You will notice that around the late 90s, millions of digital business started in America, and were able to thrive. With its improved service delivery, steeper technology learning curve, higher customer expectations, technology evolved rapidly. An e-commerce website designed in early 2000 is now superseded by self-improving product placement that evolves beyond our ability to understand, highly intelligent recommendations engines, algorithmic fraud detection, and automated fulfillment.

We can consider artificial intelligence as a new obstacle to entrepreneurs as well as an enabler.

Now, we can assume that in the next decade, the traditional careers we know would be replaced, and the ones left will have to rely on artificial intelligence to get their job done efficiently, and effectively. Entrepreneurs need to conceptualize and understand how artificial intelligence works, and how it can be applied in a new way, in order to innovate.

With the advent of artificial intelligence, entrepreneurs can leverage on modern machine learning as a service on demand with pre-trained machine learning models, cloud computers, as well as storage. There will be inherent benefits to new startups as companies continue to integrate machine learning into their businesses. Smarter CRM tools such as Hubspot and SalesForce can help improve customer service, marketing automation, and sales. These, including other platforms, will help maximize waste with well-informed decisions, maximize resources, and help optimize business timing.

Role of a Product Manager

Someone who understands the larger business objectives a feature or product will fulfill, and also able to identify the customer need, is what a product manager means. He or she must also be able to rally a team to transform the vision of the product into reality, which is in addition to articulating what success looks like for the product.

The quandary of who a product manager is developed from the novelty of the role, where those who are into crafts, such as engineering and design have been able to separate themselves through their specialization. Product managers are still giving a second look at what their role should be.

Founder of product Tank, and product leader extraordinaire, Martin Eriksson, initially explained product management in a Venn diagram, that positions product managers at the intersection of user experience, technology, and business. CEO of Opsware, Ben Horowitz, tagged product managers as "The CEO of the product." That was several years back.

I will go with Horowitz and Eriksson, but not with the way their definition is interpreted. When most people observe Eriksson's diagram, what comes across to them is product manager sand-witched between three disciplines, which are business, technology, and UX. Although, he mentioned that some of the burdens on product managers have to learn to balance the three needs, go for hard decisions, as well as trade-offs. From the analogy of Horowitz, people feel product managers are entrusted with some kind of distinct authority. They are not. But, a product manager, like a CEO, defines success, sets the goals, and helps motivate teams, and will take responsibility for the outcome.

Responsibility of a product manager

Depending on the size of the organization, some responsibilities vary. For example, in larger organizations, product managers are usually integrated with a team of specialists. Ranging from marketers, analysts, and researchers, help to gather input while designers and developers manage the daily implementation, find bugs, test prototypes, and also draw-up designs. Usually, product managers are encircled with help from different departments, but most of their time is expended on aligning their stakeholders in support of a specific vision.

Product managers in smaller organizations, on the other hand, expend a smaller amount of time getting everyone to support their idea, but spend more time, doing hands-on work that accompanies being clear about a vision, and also seeing it through.

Generally, an excellent product manager will expend his or her time on different tasks. That is,

- Establishing a shared brain across bigger teams, in order to promote independent decision making.
- Prioritizing capabilities, and product features
- Convincing stakeholder to align with the product's vision
- Crafting a vision for a product
- Developing competitive analyses and monitoring the market
- Representing and understanding user needs

Product owner vs product manager

When it comes to what a product manager does, whether or not a team is adhering to a certain agile practice, can further muddy the water. For example, a team needs to have a product owner, if they are practicing Scrum.

While the product owner works more closely with the development team to implement against the goals that the product manager helps define, the product manager defines the direction of the product through prioritization, alignment, vision-setting, and research.

This is how they break out:

Product manager

- Functions at a conceptual level
- Owns vision, marketing, ROI
- Outlines what success looks like
- Helps to define the product vision
- Works with an outside stakeholder

Product owner

- Involved in day-to-day activities
- Owns team backlog and fulfillment work
- Outline the plan for achieving success
- Helps teams execute on a shared vision
- Works with internal stakeholder

When team practices shifts, and makeups, responsibilities can shift. For example, the product manager might end-up doing the prioritization for the development team and play a larger role in ensuring that everyone is on the same page if the team isn't doing Scrum (say, they are doing Kanban or something else). The product owner often ends up taking on some of the product manager's responsibility, if a team is doing Scrum on the other hand, but doesn't have a product manager.

These can make work become really quick and murky, which is the reason team need to clearly outline responsibilities, or get prone to falling into the old ways of developing software, where a group can codify the requirements and dump it for other groups to develop. Time gets wasted, expectations get misaligned, teams run the risk of creating features or product that won't satisfy customer need when this happens.

Being a great product manager

One of the most interesting things about being a product manager is that there is no single way of doing it, just as there isn't any one kind of team. The craft has increased during the last two decades, both in approach and popularity. Product managers as a whole are still wrestling with how to label their different strengths, compared to some designers who have restricted themselves to relating with motion designers, graphic designers, and so on.

To make matters complicated, the pursuit of product management as a discipline is just gaining momentum. Although the younger generation are starting their careers with product management in mind, the older generation "fell into the discipline" from marketing, finance, or engineering.

Having said that, as a product manager, there are important skills that must be developed to enhance your productivity.

Develop a thick skin

It will inevitably make people unhappy making tradeoffs. The secret is to make the right trade-off first and develop the capacity to explain why you went for the decision. Someone can still not like it if you are good at explaining your decision, but often, you will be respected for the way you made it. Great product managers have a way of dealing with it, even if they don't.

Know how to influence without authority

One can acquire influence through many forms. Understanding how people are influenced, and listening to people is the first step. The second step is figuring how you will get them on board. It will take you a long way to become a master storyteller, even when you don't have data to back-up your points. You need to understand that until some people see the work, they won't believe you. The key to leading without any direct authority is understanding which levers to pull with which person.

Your team should be empowered to make decisions

Every decision can't be made by a product manager. The busy schedule of a product manager won't permit him or her to attend to every need. They mostly have unread messages, double or triple booked, and all of their days could be spent answering unending questions.

It is worthy of note that it is not the job of a product manager to touch every decision. By creating a shared brain- or a way of making decisions and a set of criteria for escalating them, a great product manager can empower his or her team to make their own decisions. Excellent product managers build that context.

Know what's on ground

Better than anyone, product managers need to know the lay of the land. Product managers are dropped into something that already has momentum, very rarely. They will make bad decisions if they start executing without taking the time to get their bearing.

Great product managers start by asking questions and pump the brakes. Take the first couple of months to talk to as many internal stakeholders as you can if you are just starting a product management job. A good product manager will understand the business model. He or she will also strive to understand how different people are influenced, the history of the product, etc. This is what will enable a product manager to make few decisions on their own.

Ruthlessly prioritize

The common thing between a product manager, and a politician, is that they have allotted resources to expend, and their roles require them to make good use of their resources. In order to achieve a larger goal, having in mind that they won't be able to satisfy everyone. The product manager, at some point, may have to decide between maintaining a product's default features or steering on a new path to broaden its reach and set in syn with the general business goals; a feature that might make one big customer happy but upset 100 smaller customers; or probably to beam attention on the shiny and bright or the boring and important.

What guides a product manager is clearly understanding the benefits and costs of each choice towards the right decision.

Excellent product managers

Finding a great product manager is rare. A great product manager will do all the aforementioned, and develop an excellent version of the product. It's the ability to walk people through the rationale behind a decision and convince them-- even without data, the rare forward-thinking ability, and their influence. When you think about people in this category, you will think about Steve Jobs and Elon Musk.

In part, these people are idolized because it's satisfying to put a name on a big accomplishment. But great product managers are not made by a single great thinker 99 percent of the time. They consist of a team of great people doing excellent work. The duty of a product manager is to develop his or her unique way of directing and guiding that work.

Improving Team Communication

It is essential that in an ideal workplace, communication between employees must be professional, friendly, and open. Effective communication allows work to be executed faster as key players would be duly informed of their responsibilities and roles. Also in such a setting, questions would be attended to very fast, and like impeccable clockwork, all of the cogs would run smoothly.

However, it is worthy of note that a lot of workplaces do not function on that level of efficiency. Missed deadline, misunderstanding, arguments, all constitute a bit of stress for everyone. Whichever way or form it takes, ideal communication is worth working towards. Now the question: how can you get your team to act well, and improve communication?

This section of this book will offer ways in which you can improve communication in your team.

Take responsibility for mistakes

You have to be able to relate with your employee if you want to be a great manager. This can be achieved by admitting when you have done something differently and taking responsibility for decision errors made. You are showing your employees that you are just as human as they are, by confessing your flaws because everyone makes mistakes.

Do a survey, and make it anonymous

The truth is that it can be hard for team members to be honest and candid all the time in many workplaces. Consider issuing an anonymous survey to truly understand the needs and concerns of your fellow employees. People are likely to be very candid and honest when they know that their opinion is anonymous. Invite your associates to voice their opinion on how to deal with general situations and address any concern you are aware of, as well as help, bring up issues you may not be aware of.

Utilize mobile device to your advantage

Almost everyone has a smartphone, or a smart device these days. We are all familiar with the need to have information instantly available. It is therefore reasonable to take advantage of the opportunities offered by technological advancement. There are some project management software that enables project managers to stay on top of their project progress on the go. A good old-fashioned text message is a quick and easy way to get in contact, with those behind on time.

Be honest and open with your team member

Be honest and open with your team members, and let them know that they can also do the same with you. In any relationship, including a professional one, mutual trust is very important.

Instilling a sense of trust among your team members is possibly the single most effective way to improve interpersonal communication in the workplace. Here, transparency is important. Any trust you have built goes right out of the window if team members feel like secrets are being kept from them. Even though sensitive information should be kept as such, you have to inform your team members if they don't have access to that information.

Recognize the strength of the individuals in your team, and use them to your advantage

Understand that we don't communicate the same way. Auditory people benefit more from a phone call, video chat, or face-to-face meetings, while visual people tend to prefer written forms of communication(cloud-based software, or email). When you respect differences, it will not only send the message to your team members that you value them as individuals and recognizing the best form of communication that works best for them, it also allows for better communication. When you value a team member, he or she will be ready and willing to go beyond and above for the company.

Pay attention to diversity issues

Unique ideas come together to create something truly special when people of all nationalities, ideologies, races, and language collaborates. Cultural colloquialism, dialect, nuances, accents can make clear communication difficult. Team leaders first need to recognize that the problem is indeed a problem to combat these difficulties. It doesn't help anyone sweeping these kinds of issues under the rug, even though they may be comfortable to address for some. Make it a point to discuss ways to overcome the obstacles present, and be open with your team members about the problem at hand.

Support any group leader you identify

There are several leaders and main leaders that take control of smaller groups, in most projects. It is easier to for team members to know who to go to in the event of a problem or question when you make it clear from the start who those leaders are. Delegating roles to others shares the work equally among leaders and cut down the stress on each of the team members.

For more transparency, utilize project management software

For good reason, it seems, everyone, these days is switching to software and cloud-based storage. Cloud-based project management software enables transparency across board, allowing every team member to be able to track their progress, as well as work with other members, and confirm project details and due dates. Everyone has access to the specifics of the project and the ability to leave comments for others to see, with one streamlined system.

Note the best form of communication you can recognize

You can't communicate the same in all situations. A video conference is an excellent way for everyone to keep in contact about progress and milestones, for projects involving team members working remotely. One-to-one meetings are often the best method of communication, for in-house projects. In the past few decades, email has been a popular form of contact, but sometimes, it can be unreliable and efficient. Emails can get lost in transit, overlooked in a crowded inbox, or sent to the junk folder.

Your team will reset with communication training

Communication training is very effective in helping to improve the communication of your team. Communication training goes beyond basic conversational skills. It could include presentation skills, managerial skills training, business writing, etc, depending on the course. These courses can be expensive, but the advantage is more than the cost when your team is operating at an optimal level.

Have a purpose for your coffee breaks

A set coffee break for all employees together allows everyone to interact informally while still in the workplace, keeping in the spirit of team-building. What gets most people through the day is coffee, as it serves as fuel. So you can make the drinking productive and enjoyable at the same time. A study has revealed that discussion on coffee, whether it relates to work or not, encourages the exchange of ideas, and healthy communication among co-workers.

Have fun together to increase your mood

An escape room is one of the activities that encourages teamwork, informal, and fun interaction. A lot of cities have these, and even reduce the price for some workgroup. Coworkers naturally communicate better, when they are comfortable around each other. Most people work harder towards a common goal and build a strong sense of reciprocity when they have the feeling of having a "work family."

Over the years, team-building techniques have been employed to improve the communication among team members. Get the group together and play cards, but rather than role-playing, or any of those other workplace activities that no one actually likes. Once in a month, you can host an after-work pizza party, and play different games.

Be specific about tasks so that your team members can know their responsibility clearly

If your team members are unsure of what tasks they are responsible for, no one can effectively complete an assignment. Ensure that your team member understands their scope of project, and that they are very clear about their responsibilities, and what is expected of them. Another good way to keep everyone on track and assure that all team members are aware of their responsibilities in the project is getting the team together regularly to address any issue, ask questions, and check progress.

Be accepting of feedback

Criticisms are meant to be constructive. It is important that it be clear to all parties involved, in order to get the most out of feedback. To all parties involved, constructive criticism is important. Just a plain "fix this" in response to a submitted project can't be helpful to anyone. Feedback needs to be clear and detailed for it to be effective. It can also be documented for other people to work on it. You also have to be able to accept feedback. At some point in our lives, we all need constructive feedback, because no one is perfect.

Operate an open door policy. It encourages trust

When you operate an open door policy, it communicates that anyone can enter your space to ask you questions, pitch ideas at any time, and voice concerns. This is very essential in helping to solidify trust in your team. When you operate a closed-door policy, it sends the wrong message to lower or middle-level employees that you are not accessible. It is crucial to keep the door of your office widely open.

You can bring your team together, improve communication, and generally make the workplace a more enjoyable and stress-free place to be by utilizing some, or all of these tips. These factors promote better control over the budget and increased satisfaction from clients, and improve project quality. Cohesiveness is translated to your team being at its most productive when the workplace becomes a second home, and co-workers become a second family.

The New Categories of Entrepreneurs

The late 90s were about Harvard MBA, applying traditional management techniques to leverage on brand new internet technologies, which is already gaining momentum. As a result, the previous decades experienced a similar shift in the characterizations of entrepreneurs. Now is a new decade, we are witnessing a new category of entrepreneurship motivated by industry executives with deep product knowledge and background, who are leveraging on the power of technology to disrupt a traditionally non-tech industry. The "aughts" introduced the "22-year-old Computer Science" graduate applying technology to a low hanging industry.

It is difficult to imagine that it has just been less than 11 years since the release of the first pervasive smartphone, but its positive effects can't be denied in this ever-changing world. With the launch of the iPhone in April 2007, Apple changed everything. An equally important phenomenon emerged, outside the development of a new dimension of industry-driven, by service, location-based, (and with a myriad of billion-dollar companies). In addition to doctors, car mechanics, lawyers, and professionals from every sector of the economy having a tool for productivity, they also have a piece of technology handy that they embrace as an intimate, which have become a very important part of their lives. Everyone around the world has started embracing technology as more than just a work tool, by developing a technology that was intuitive to the consumer masses.

It is now part of our trends, moving forward; particularly the executives in the industry will be the next category of in-demand start-up CEO, and it gradually changing how we will perceive entrepreneurs. This has opened-up a multi-trillion dollar economy that is opening up to technology faster than we have ever thought or imagined.

Further, you may have heard, on several occasions, a discussion between construction workers, saying *"We should be able to do.....if we have an app for...."* Quite unfortunate, this type of conversation is far from the Silicon Valley's ears, which are swept by the talk of what will be the next Twitter or Instagram. A new category of entrepreneurs is emerging even with that. That is a category of entrepreneurs, who see the challenges in the industry, firsthand, and also the opportunity to make a world-changing impact.

Paradigm shift initiated by this category of entrepreneur

We are currently in a generation where a group of young individuals or even a single individual now believes that they have the capacity to solve complex problems on their own. This increases interest in entrepreneurship, particularly among the younger generations, which has developed into three major implications for large companies; with the increased access to capital, low barrier to entry, and reduced risk as far as getting back into job tracks are concerned. These implications will be discussed shortly.

You must understand that entrepreneurship is not only restricted to businesses. As a result of the inspiration derived by Steve Jobs and the popularity of very successful young role models like Elon Musk, Evans Spiegel Mark Zuckerberg, Phanindra Sama, etc, the new category of entrepreneurship is not showing any sign of slowing down soon, particularly among the younger generation who are the biggest enabler of this entrepreneurship movement.

Further, there are specialized tools like Lean Start-up, Business Model Canvas, as well as Design Thinking to aid aspiring entrepreneurs to create and develop their ideas in a very organized manner. Accelerators and Incubators are mushrooms everywhere in the world, from Cordoba in Argentina to Kochi in India.

Human Resources department has to re-sketch the future of work:
A research conducted by the Global Shapers Community, a circle of young leaders with high potentials between the age range of 20-29, revealed that these young people created opportunities to make a difference to society as the most important thing they look for in a job. It is for this reason that HR Leaders need to restructure their job descriptions, organizational culture, as well as constant training to be able to benefit from the unending trend.

Take for example Jaideep Bansalm who is a Global Innovation Shaper from the Chandigarh Hub. After completing his mechanical engineering degree from the Indian Institute of Technology, Mumbai, he works for a leading multinational corporation in India. It is worthy of note that Jaideep joined the Global Himalayan Expedition to install an education-based infrastructure, and sustainable energy and in the remote Himalayan regions. When the project was about to commence, Jaideep and his other team members of GHE trekked along a mountain at fourteen thousand feet for more than two days to reach a village that never has seen electricity, transporting some solar equipment on the back of a horse.

After arriving at their destination, the team was able to successfully electrify the village after experiencing a grueling journey to the Himalayas. The village danced and celebrated and that special moment in their history, and Jaideep experienced the most fulfilling time of his life. It was that impact and inspiration he got from the experience that led him to take two months sabbatical, and repeat the expedition to six other villages at over 14,000ft in the Himalayas.

Now it begs the question: how do we plan to involve the likes of Jaideep of this generation to the world, who are interested in taking up challenges of the world? In order for employees to be able to pursue some of their passions that allows them the entrepreneurial kick, an organization like SAP are now encouraging their workers to undertake a social sabbatical because it is crucial that companies are able to figure out how to integrate more purpose into their job descriptions. In addition to looking for jobs that can give much more purpose to their lives, very talented young people are now looking for organizations with a good purpose.

It is no longer news that the archaic approaches to governing and managing employee-related-concerns are gradually fading, thus as a result, HR teams have to devise brand new ways to further and be able to connect the dot in their "divided-approach" existing between generation Y and generation Z, to establish entrepreneurship as a way of life. HR must be able to integrate and recognize exceptional and young talents into their boards of their trustees to deconstruct the status quo at the top and facilitate an entrepreneurial environment.

Eileen Guo is the founder of the Norfolk hub, which is located in the United States of America In a bid to launch Impassion Media, she went to Afghanistan some time back. The organization is the first Afghanistan's digital media agencies. In the year, 2013, she brought together more than 200 of Afghanistan's social media users from 24 provinces and abroad for the country's first-ever social media summit, aimed at promoting the use of social media around the country. Living in Afghanistan means that she has lived in one of the most difficult conditions, incubating a new business, and creating a new frontier. You could imagine how that would have been.

Eileen learned some lessons while she was in Afghanistan, which come with a lot of enriching insights into building an eco-system to target non-consumers, building and operating new businesses in such complex settings, designing for extremes-- with all being of great value to any business leader. HR departments must be innovative and think of ways that mentoring programs can be designed in a bid to increase the value of their top team members, such that they would be able to offer more value, and enriching experience as well as insight from gifted and sharp young minds. Eileen is a good example.

Entrepreneurship is being redefined in every industry, and young people are the force pushing this movement. Bringing together young talents, and understanding the implication, through creative business models, and re-strategizing on how different departments within organizations can capture values from this important trend-- is crucial to the long-term success of any corporation, seeking global relevance.

Connecting the "divided-approach" between Generation Y and Generation Z. Organizations have to continually think of a way they can create an entrepreneurial culture in their organizations to stay in unison with the needs of the young people who look for entrepreneurial challenges. Although the traditional training is still relevant, however, HR must also invest heavily in its top executives to learn the young person's way of doing things.

Revisiting the scope of marketing: In addition to improving "Customer Relationship Management" Marketing departments also have to include and improve "Community Management." To achieve this, they will have to develop skills that are mostly developed by working in government as they now have to developed policies, guidelines, rules of engagement, and be available all the time.

Autodesk owns a 3D animation software, named Maya. This software employed the use of special plugins to help animators in their work. Maya went further to assemble the best among the best plugins as a regular feature into all of their software, which has proved to be one of the most widely used software in the animation industry. In the case of Apple's Maya, value creation comes to life with the help of community power facilitated by an open business model. In addition to managing entrepreneurial communities, the marketers need to solidify value through online communities, and created platforms such as Nike and Jawbone, and learn to also manage the fury of clients, who pour out their anger on or through social media or whenever they are experiencing poor service.

Organizations, such as Apple once created an online forum that capitalized on the power of peer networks to find solutions to routine problems faced by customers, and consequently created value for both the company, as well as the customers. As time progresses, the iPad /iPhone platform allows small companies and individual developers to develop apps and kick-started the iOs developer communities.

In a way, one of the biggest shift in the marketer's role is the introduction of community management as a key function, and the success of a marketing manager lies in his or her ability to manage and engage communities in both the real and also the virtual worlds in order to be able to create meaningful value for the company, and also the customers. Therefore, as business models become more open, marketing departments need to adapt and change.

Business structures have to be more open: One of the ways most organizations are leveraging on these young talents and ideas is by creating an open innovation model in areas that are very strategic to the company. Big organizations can leverage on the linkage between them and start-ups. While large companies can take proven business models to the last mile because of their scale and reach, start-ups succeed in creating ways for the first mile of business. Networking giant, Cisco launched a new start-up innovation program popularly known as Cisco Entrepreneur in Residence EIR that positioned Cisco to directly engage and support early-stage start-ups, while working together on game-changing ideas for Big Data/Analytics, the Internet of Things, Cloud service, and other areas that are likely to be strategic to Cisco in the nearest future.

In the nearest future, it will be very challenging to attract great talents to work in large organizations. Any young talent can start and set-up anywhere in the world, thanks to the increased access to capital, which can create a breakthrough business model that is capable of disrupting large business corporations. In addition to large organizations losing top talents, they also at the risk of getting disrupted by a start-up launched by these young talents.

Organizations like Johnson & Johnson, Unilever, and so on, organize their own VC arms that invest in promising start-ups in their strategic focus areas. Cisco aims to connect the formerly unconnected world, and see the future direction of its industry, and also an opportunity to co-create new business models with their engagement and collaboration with start-ups. This also helps Cisco to know the trend that is affecting their business model and prepare to defend against the disruption. Large organizations also partner with incubators and accelerators to stay close to start-ups.

Various challenges and issues were identified and addressed by past winners of the program such as developing myoelectric prosthetic limbs for disabled women and children living in rural areas in Kolkata, tracking crime patterns for a safer culture in Puebia, women in Phnom Penh, Rabat, and empowering young people, and generating electricity through solar in Nairobi. "Open" models are gradually becoming mainstream in different industries. Companies can use these models to prepare to defend against disruption, send employees to training, and bring back the start-up culture into their organization.

An example that reveals what gives an insight into what issues young people care about in different part of the world and allow them to design their sustainability strategies in tune with the realities of the world, was when Coca Cola, The Global Community Partners of the Global Shapers Community, and The Abraaj launched an annual global challenge inviting scalable models from Global Shapers and supporting the winner with a seed fund.

Coordinating Your Team Efforts

The new generations of (young) managers believe that multitasking is the name of the game now. For some strange reasons, they feel like they won't move far up the corporate ladder if they don't demonstrate superior multitasking abilities,

This is a completely bad way of managing teams and it often causes poor customer experience, delays, and low performance.

First of all, no matter how efficient it might be, one person can only achieve a limited number of things in a single day. An attempt to go beyond the limits means compromising on the quality and burning out because, consequently, none of those tasks will be done with impeccable efficiency, and besides, there won't be enough time.

Secondly, if you are multitasking, your team is either idling or fighting with confusion since you are taking bits and pieces of their tasks so now they are not sure how and from where to continue.

Now try to picture Elon Musk, waking up early on a hot sunny day, while running to get coffee, the mail; then going to his company just to put together a part of the propulsion system, and get back and attend to a few meetings before he hit the laptop to reply some billions of emails he received in last few hours. And, mind you, that's just in the first two hours of his day. He will definitely be overwhelmed.

It doesn't work like that. A leader is a leader because he or she has the responsibility to motivate and coordinate; nothing more. For instance, Winters, commander of the 2nd battalion, Major Richard D., 506th Parachute Infantry Regiment of the 101st Airborne Division, had spent the second half of his deployment in WWII on the front lines - unarmed! You couldn't see him firing mortars, digging trenches, and flinging hand grenades while running around to maintain uninterrupted communication between the platoons and companies. He only has the responsibility to lead.

The same can also be said of micromanaging. You'll micromanage If you want to induce confusion. You'll step aside and let people do their job as Major Richard did if you want to run a high-performing team. Remember that the reason you hired a professional in the first place is for you to be able to delegate with ease.

Managers Manage, Leader Lead

As an employer, you should be like a guiding angel that watches over your employees from the place they don't have access to, even to the physical places. Your ruling is total and undisputed in their minds, and they have this yearn to come in close contact with you, anxious to get encouraged; and a pat on the back that will confirm that their sacrifice and effort is satisfying his greatness, the supreme leader, which is you.

Think about how an entry-level assembly worker will feel when Elon walks by, and pats his back, saying: "Weldone. Good job." The worker doesn't even need to be paid for that month. A single show of gratitude from Elon Musk would suffice for him to work harder and happily.

It is worthy of note that you are predominantly a leader, as an entrepreneur. Your responsibility is to hire, inspire and manage so that he or she could help you achieve the vision you have for your organization by developing strategies (mission) and setting series of achievable goals both in the short and long term.

You need to note that there's a distinct difference between the two concepts. A manager helps to deliver immediate results based on a proposed vision, whereas, a leader conveys the vision to inspire teams. Said in another way, a manager has people working for him, while a leader has a tribe of raving followers.

Positioning Yourself As an Expert In Your Field

Becoming an expert gives you the power to influence and control, which directly grows your followership. When you are knowledgeable in a field, it has the capacity of skyrocketing the profits of your business, as well as landing you incredible opportunities in your industry. You need to strive to position yourself as someone knowledgeable in your desired industry. You can now see clearly the reason why positioning yourself as an expert can enhance your image and also business? These are a few ways in which you can trail to position yourself as an expert in your industry:

● Push your publication on authority media platforms: This means applying to be a guest writer or speaker on a media platform through their email or contact address. What this approach does is give you social proof that you are actually an expert in your industry. This can be both print and electronic media platforms.

● Become a member of your industry association: This gives you a kind of authentication that you are legit, and also help you build trust and credibility with your audience. Most industries have an association or membership, that can make you connect with other experts in your field. What this also means is that you are aware of and committed to the standards of the industry.

● Highlight your expertise and note some testimonials: If you don't have any testimonials yet, you can consider asking your mentor or past employer to write a testimonial about you. If you have helped people to solve their problems with your knowledge. You can highlight them on or with whatever platform you deem fit.

● Get invites to relevant podcasts related to your field: You can build authority by telling your story and sharing your knowledge as a guest on a podcast. Whatever knowledge you will be sharing must be something that will make you appeal to the audience. That means you need to understand who your audience is. The host of the podcast will introduce you as an expert in the industry you belong to.

- Always endeavor to offer some unique perspective: What will differentiate yours from others is the unique perspective you offer to your audience. This is also known as becoming a "thought" leader. Your perspective could be a twist on a specific topic, or maybe you have studied popular opinions and you feel yours can change people's perspective. There are many contents about your industry. Whatever topic you want to write about, it is important that you make it interesting and memorable.

- Consistency is key in writing and speaking about your expertise: To achieve this, you must be consistent about creating content in your industry and publish it on a website, blog, or all of your social media platforms. Writing more about your expertise will make people remember you whenever they see or hear you about your industry. Consistency is an important element of positioning as an expert.

- It is essential that you update your marketing messaging: Words like specialist, expert, skilled, professional, trained, qualified, certified, talented, award-winning, competent, proficient, authority, etc are some of the words you could use. Think of words that show that you as an expert, and also the words that describe the market you are targeting. Highlight these words in your profile and messaging, and use them on your various social media.

- It is important that you have good experience and knowledge in the industry you would like to be an expert in: There are free online courses you enroll for and books online that you could read. If you don't have a college degree, you can get the required knowledge to equip yourself with your industry knowledge on the internet.

Effective Data Management

Data management is gradually becoming the support system of a good online marketing strategy, as digital marketing evolves. Having reliable, quality and clean data that reveals a profound insight in your customer behavior pattern and data are very crucial to creating marketing automation and campaign that properly nurture your leads and transform them into buying customers.

You must follow these data management best practices to ensure your company's data is quality. Or else, you may end-up with impure data that elicits issues with your marketing automation, and campaign targeting.

Here are some of the best practices for managing your data effectively:

List out your business goals

When it comes to data management, you don't want to jump straight into the deep end. Take a baby step by outlining exactly the goal you want to see for your company's data. You can keep the information that is relevant to your goal when you know what you plan to do with the data you collect. It also ensures that your data management software is not unorganized and overcrowded.

You are helping to keep your data management software, well by keeping only the data that your company is going to use. These are some goals examples that your business might have:
- Train marketing and sales team on data use
- Find customers buying pattern/habits
- Creating a buyer profile/audience targeting
- Create/improve automation and processes
- Improve decision-making

Of course, there is an end list of things you could do with your data, but the most important thing is to commence by listing out your goals. For you not to end up with tons of data that is completely irrelevant to your company's needs, your business data goal will direct your data management process.

Prioritize your data security and protection

To ensure that your company doesn't fall victim, and endanger the information of your entire customer base, as well as a data breach, this is an essential step to take. And it should be the first thing. If there is anything that has been gleaned from media platforms like Facebook, it is that people are not cool with an unknown third party gaining access to their personal data. When it comes to your business's data management, data protection and security need to be a number one priority.

A few years back, the General Data Protection Regulation GDPR came up, and it not only affected businesses that market and sell to customers that reside within the EU but also all businesses that operate within the EU, with other nations likely to do the same in no long distance. To ensure the privacy of your leads and customers, it is crucial for your company to follow all applicable guidelines.

Complying with GDPR plus other regulations when it comes to collecting data can improve your data protection. Also, proper data management software can help ensure the safety and security of your data. Ensure that your team members know how to handle the data they work with properly, by putting the right people in charge of your data management.

Lastly, If there is a suspected data breach within your company, you have to come up with some course of action to take or plan. This won't happen ideally, but you have to have some strategy in place to handle such a situation.

Pay attention to your data

There are also many steps you can take to ensure that the data your company is collecting is reliable and clean. As aforementioned, a great way to improve data quality is limiting your data to only the necessary information your company needs to meet its goals.

First of all, data can become irrelevant and outdated to your sales and marketing teams, this is why data must be regularly checked for accuracy. Stale or outdated data should be removed from your data management software. This is to prevent it from having a negative impact on processes within your marketing and sales department, analytics, and automation.

Training all team members who have access to the data about the proper ways to collect and input data is another step to take to help your team focus on data quality within your data management. Training is important when you have team members setting up these automation or instances where data may be manually added to your data management software or CRM. Although, most ways are likely to be automated. This prevents data from being inputted incorrectly, thereby preventing it in the future.

Before data is used for reporting or analytic purpose to improve the accuracy of all metrics pulled from said data, ensure that data it is checked and ascertained clean. Placing data quality as a top priority, and also data security helps to keep every aspect of the organization's data reliable and clean.

Cut down duplicate data

It is essential for your company to have a way of handling these potential redundancies. There are scores of approaches that your company can employ to reduce duplicate data from a lead customer. Ensure your company has processes in place to avoid duplicate data being added to your data management system, if a customer is returning to make another purchase, or offers.

When first setting up their data, many companies may not think about this. It is therefore important to have a system in place that allows data to be checked or updated when someone makes a return purchase and opts in more than once. Another way to ensure your data stays clean is by putting in precautions when it comes to duplicate data and redundancies.

It is crucial for your data to be accessible to your team

When it comes to accessing your data, the line between convenience and security is very slim. Your data protection policy should be such that a person without permission shouldn't be able to gain access to your customer's data, and ensure that those on your marketing and sales team have access to this information, for them to be able to do their daily job.

Based on their specific roles, it is a smart idea to set up particular logins and access permission for your employees or co-workers. Team leaders and executives who need to access customers' data than sales representatives or analysts need to have more permission than individuals who only require some types of data. This helps to ensure that customers' data are protected within your company. Having different permission levels simplifies things for your team member, and allow them the necessary data, as against trying to secure your permissions and blanket rules that can cause issues, be too open in some cases, and be restrictive in others.

Have a strategy to recover your data

Anything can happen anytime. It is therefore important that your company has a strategy to recover lost data because accidents happen anytime. Losing your customers' data will negatively affect your sales strategy, marketing automation, and your marketing campaigns. You need to have a backup or recovery plan in place if your CRM or data management software were to go under, if your account were to somehow get shut down, or if someone were to make a mistake and delete some or all your data.

It is therefore advisable to have a solution in place for your business, in case issues of missing data occurs. You can upload the file to a cloud service like Google Drive or Dropbox, or try exporting your data so that you still have a file with all the information saved on a hard drive. In case you get locked out, ensure that your security account has secret permissions in place. If anything happens, create a back up of all data so that you can quickly and easily restore it.

Invest in a quality data management software

One of the most important steps to managing your data effectively is finding good data management software. There is a lot that goes into finding the perfect data management software for your needs, whether it is too large of a system for your business needs (some data management companies only focus on enterprise companies rather than businesses of all shapes and size), or to complex for your team to understand, or not secure enough for your business to feel comfortable relying on.

You want to lay hands on a data platform that helps you engage with your audience in a precise and timely manner, or that is going to give you clear and accurate insight into your leads and customers' data. By automatically cleaning the data, and enriching the data to ensure that you have the most complete and accurate view of your data possible, your customer data platform should be making the job of your marketing and sales seems easier.

You are putting your organization into unnecessary spending, by relearning a new system, retraining their staff on how to properly input data, and redesigning a new process surrounding data input if you invest in the wrong customer data platform right off the bat.

The Transformation of Artificial Intelligence on Business

On a daily basis, you probably interact with artificial intelligence. A lot of people still consider artificial intelligence as fiction dystopias, but the characterization is reducing as artificial intelligence becomes more commonplace and developed in our daily lives. However, today, artificial intelligence has become a household name.

It is not a new concept, even though artificial intelligence appears to mainstream society as a new phenomenon. In the year 1956, the modern field of artificial intelligence came into existence, but it, however, took years of work, and significant progress towards making artificial intelligence system and making it a technological reality and continually develop it.

Artificial intelligence has a wide range of use in business. In some form or another, a lot of us interact with artificial intelligence. Artificial intelligence is already disrupting virtually every business process in every industry, from the mundane to the breathtaking. Artificial intelligence is becoming imperative for businesses that want to maintain a competitive edge, as the technologies proliferate.

What do you understand as artificial intelligence

It is important to define the term "Artificial Intelligence" before examining how artificial intelligence technologies are impacting the business world. AI is a general and very broad term that refers to a kind of software that has the nature of humans, which includes problem-solving, planning, and learning. Naming specific applications, Artificial Intelligence can be compared to calling a 2020 Range Rovers a "car"-- you are technically correct if that is what you call it. But it doesn't touch on any specific. We have to dig deeper to understand what type of artificial intelligence is predominant.

Machine Learning

In the development of businesses today, machine learning is one of the most common types of artificial intelligence. When it comes to processing a large amount of data very fast, then you can count on machine language. When you feed a machine learning algorithm with more data, its modeling improves. Such artificial intelligence is algorithms that appear to learn in a space of time, and they become better by it the more they do it. You need machine learning to go through vast troves of data-- captured by linking the Internet of Things and devices into understandable language for humans.

For instance, your company is likely hooked up to the network if you manage a manufacturing plant. When devices are connected, it feeds a constant stream of data production, data, and more to a central location. However, this is too much data for humans to handle, and even if humans could, the most important pattern would be missing. One of the important functionality of machine learning is that it can rapidly identify patterns and anomalies, and analyze data as they come in. A machine learning algorithm can catch it and notify decision-makers that it is time to dispatch a preventive maintenance team if a machine in the manufacturing plant is working at a reduced capacity.

It is worthy of note that the development of an interconnected web of artificial intelligence "nodes," artificial neural networks, has paved way for what is known as deep learning.

Business Today and Artificial Intelligence

Artificial intelligence is generally seen as a supporting tool, rather than serving as a replacement for human intelligence and ingenuity. Artificial intelligence is adept at processing and analyzing troves of data far more quickly than a human brain could, although in the real world, artificial intelligence sometimes has issues in executing commonsense tasks. Artificial intelligence software is capable of returning synthesized strings of action and offer them to the human user. This will enable human users to be able to streamline the decision-making process and help game out possible consequences of each action.

The founder and CEO of machine learning company SparkCognition, Amir Husain said, *"Artificial intelligence is kind of the second coming software. It is a form of software that makes decisions on its own, that's able to act even in situations not foreseen by the programmers. Artificial intelligence has a wider latitude of decision-making ability as opposed to traditional software."*

Whether it is performing a task as complex as monitoring a wind turbine to predict when it will need repairs, or just by assisting both staffs and visitors navigate their way in the corporate campus, efficiently, these traits make artificial intelligence highly valuable throughout many industries. Only systems that capture a large amount of data can be used with artificial intelligence. For instance, a smart energy management system helps to collect information from sensors affixed to different assets. This data are then put in context by machine learning algorithms, and transferred to human decision-makers to be able to understand energy maintenance and usage demands.

When it comes to looking for holes in computer network defenses, artificial intelligence is even an indispensable ally. According to Husain *"You really can't have enough cybersecurity experts to look at these problems, because of scale and increasing complexity. Artificial intelligence is playing an increasing role here as well."*

Customer Relationship Management, CRM, is also changing as a result of artificial intelligence. Software such as Zoho and Salesforce needs human intervention to remain accurate and up to date. A normal CRM system transforms into auto-correcting, a self-updating system that stays on top of your relationship management for you.

The versatility of artificial intelligence is also reflected in the financial sector. Visiting professor at the Massachusetts Institute of Technology, founder and CEO of artificial intelligence concierge company Flybit, Dr. Hassein Rahnama, worked with TD Bank to integrate artificial intelligence into regular banking operations, such as mortgage loans.

Rahnama said *"using this technology, if you have a mortgage with the bank and it's up for renewal in 90 days or less ... if you're walking by a branch, you get a personalized message inviting you to go to the branch and renew purchase."* He furthered by saying *"If you are looking at a property for sale and you spend more than 10 minutes there, it will send you a possible mortgage offer. We are no longer expecting the user to constantly be on a search box Googling what they need. The paradigm is shifting as to how the right information finds the right user at the right time."*

Final Thoughts

If a future entrepreneur is born today, he would likely graduate from college around 2040. Then the advancement of artificial intelligence and technology would have exponentially increased. Future entrepreneurs must understand it in order to innovate with it.

This is why it is crucial for artificial intelligence literacy to be integrated into the school curriculum, to oil the mind of the young and talented future entrepreneur. With the historically slow pace of change in education and faster adoption curves, now is the time to act, before too many traditional career paths vanish.